HANCOCK*fabrics*.

Fashion Fleece

Creating Polar Magic

with Nancy Cornwell

The fabric, notions and patterns featured throughout this book are available at your favorite Hancock Fabrics store or online at www.hancockfabrics.com

©2006 by Nancy Cornwell

Published by

kp **krause publications**
An Imprint of F+W Publications

700 East State Street • Iola, WI 54990-0001
715-445-2214 • 888-457-2873

Our toll-free number to place an order or obtain a free catalog is
(800) 258-0929.

Library of Congress Catalog Number: 2006905832
ISBN-13: 978-0-89689-514-0
ISBN-10: 0-89689-514-9

Edited by Maria L. Turner
Designed by Donna Mummery

Printed in the United States of America

The following are copyrighted and used throughout this book:
Mesh Transfer Canvas (Clover Needlecraft, Inc.)
Water-Soluble Pencils (Clover Needlecraft, Inc.)
Wash-Away Wonder Tape (W.H. Collins, Inc.)
Chenille by the Inch™ (Fabric Café™)
Sulky® KK2000™ (Gunold + Stykma)
Sulky® Ultra Solvy™ (Gunold + Stykma)
Olfa® Chenille Cutter (Olfa – North America)
Olfa® Decorative Wave Blade (Olfa – North America)
Olfa® Decorative Scallop Blade (Olfa – North America)
Olfa® Decorative Pinking Blade (Olfa – North America)
Olfa® Rotary Cutter (Olfa – North America)
June Tailor® Fancy Fleece™ Slotted Ruler (June Tailor, Inc.)

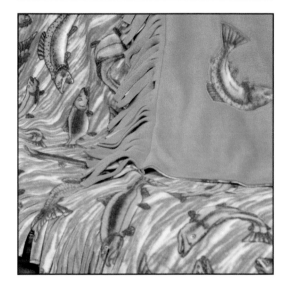

Rota...

Rota...
from s...
the st...
size w...
to use...
The lar...
handle...
the co...
handle...
use, ...
my ha...
larger ...
needs.)

Cho...
rotary ...
pinkin...
finishe...
Blunt-E...

Olfa...
edge. T...
benefi...
either ...
blade t...

June...

This ...
for use...
scallop...
spaced...
use wh...

HANCOCK *fabrics*.

Fashion Fleece

G...

Wa...

I h...
side...
choo...
¼" w...
can...
up t...
be r...
for t...
you...

Wo...
garm...
wou...
shift...
"bas...
It is...
appl...

Lor...
Flo...

Pin...
the l...
avoi...
blad...
pinn...
angl...

The Basics

Fabric and Garment Care

Pre-treating

There's no need to pre-treat fleece since fleece does not shrink or shed excess color. You can buy it and sew immediately!

Laundering

To avoid unnecessary abrasion, wash finished garments inside-out and with similar garments. Use a powdered detergent, lukewarm water and the gentle cycle. Don't use bleach or any type of softening agent (liquid or dryer sheets). Toss in the dryer on low heat for a short time.

Pressing

Pressing is not recommended on fleece. If, during the construction stage, you feel a compelling urge to press, hold the iron above the fleece and steam it. Then gently finger press to encourage the fleece to lie in the desired position. Never place an iron soleplate in direct contact with fleece. Direct contact may leave a permanent iron imprint on the fleece.

𝒩ancy's 𝒩ote

Many times you will handle a small piece of fleece (a square, a patch or an appliqué). To determine the right side of the fabric, gently pull on the cut edges in all directions of the piece. Fleece has decidedly more stretch on the crossgrain. After determining the cut edge with the most stretch, tug along that cut edge and the fleece will curl to the wrong side.

Which is the Right Side?

Always test for the right side of the fabric.

To find the right side of fleece, stretch it along the cut edge on the crossgrain (direction of most stretch). The fleece will curl to the wrong side. Remember this. You'll use it often.

General Sewing Basics

Thread

Choose good-quality, long-staple polyester thread that matches your fleece color or is a shade darker.

Needles

Always begin a project with a fresh, new needle. Because fleece is a knitted fabric, choose a universal, stretch or ballpoint needle. These needles have rounded points that deflect rather than pierce the yarn.

Choose size 70/10 or 75/11 for lightweight fleece; size 80/12 or 90/14 for medium-weight fleece; and size 100/16 for heavyweight fleece.

𝒩ancy's 𝒩ote

If you experience skipped stitches or break a needle, go up one needle size. If you are using an older, temperamental machine and experiencing skipped stitches, try using a zigzag stitch 3mm to 4mm long and .5mm to 1mm wide.

𝒩ancy's 𝒢olden 𝒭ule

Always lengthen your stitch length when sewing on fleece. Never use a stitch length shorter than 3mm (nine stitches per inch). I generally sew with a 3.5mm or 4mm stitch length. This prevents stretched or wavy seams.

6

Quick Fringe Technique

I featured this super-fast way to fringe fleece in all of my books. I am repeating it here because you will use it a lot!

MATERIALS NEEDED
Large cutting mat
Smaller cutting mat
Rotary cutter

Directions
1. Lay the fleece on the larger cutting mat.
2. Lay a smaller cutting mat on the fleece 2", 3", 4" (or whatever depth you want the fringe to be) from the end of the fleece to be fringed.
3. Fold the fleece to be fringed over the smaller mat.
4. Use the rotary cutter to cut the fringe. Cut from the smaller mat and "run" onto the larger mat.

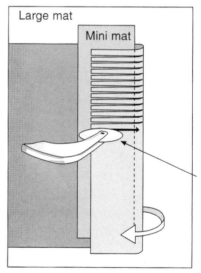

Fold over desired fringe depth.

Nancy's Note
Quick fringe can be done on one edge (bottom of a vest), two edges (opposite ends of a scarf, blanket or pillow), four edges (all sides of a blanket or pillow) and on a single layer or a double layer.

To make the blanket shown, refer to page 13 for blanket directions and page 10 for reverse appliqué directions.

Quick Fringe Basics

- Fringe-cuts can be virtually any width. The most common and most effective are fringe-cuts between ½" and 1" wide.

- Unless you have a specific design need, never cut fringe narrower than ½" when the fringe is cut on the crossgrain (fringe-cuts perpendicular to the selvage). Fringe-cuts on the crossgrain are stretchy. Narrow, stretchy fringe-cuts distort easily.

- Never cut fringe narrower than ½" on baby or toddler items. Narrower fringe can potentially break off and present a swallowing danger.

- Fringe-cuts can be virtually any length. The most common—and most effective—are between 2½" and 5" long.

- Quick fringe-cuts can be made using a straight or specialty blade rotary cutter.

- The width and length of the fringe and the choice of blade edge are governed by the end use, the fleece print and personal taste. There is no right or wrong.

MATERIALS NEEDED
Throw (54" x 60"): 1½ yards fleece
Blanket (60" x 72"): 2 yards fleece

Throw/Blanket Directions

1. Cut the fleece to the desired size.

2. Following the Quick Fringe Technique directions on pages 7, cut fringe ½" to ¾" wide and 3" to 5" long on two opposing sides of the blanket.

Nancy's Note

When only two sides of a blanket are being fringed, the fringe generally is cut on the shorter sides. However, you can fringe any two opposing sides if your print dictates otherwise. If you can't decide, quick fringe all four sides!

To maintain this beautiful print along the long edge, fringe was cut on the two short sides only.

Easy Fringed Throw

Double border print fleeces make lovely blankets and throws for a quick home dec pick-me-up. This single-layer blanket with fringe on two ends can easily go from cutting table to couch in 10 minutes! Dedicate an hour and you can make a coordinating pillow.

Pillow Directions

Refer to page 42 for materials and step-by-steps for a 16" pillow.

Reverse Appliqué Technique

Reverse appliqué on fleece is similar to traditional reverse appliqué (on woven cottons) except that when using fleece, you don't have to do the finishing steps!

Begin with two layers of fleece (like a double-layer blanket, scarf or vest). Stitch a motif and then trim away one fleece layer within the motif.

You can combine a print with a solid fleece or use two solid fleeces. Using a print fleece is, of course, the easiest. You simply have to outline stitch the printed motif.

Blanket/Throw Directions

1. Place the fleece layers with wrong sides together (finished position), stitch and finish outer edges of garment or blanket as desired.

2. Determine which print motifs you are going to highlight. These print motifs won't look much different on the print side but since they will be visible on the solid side, you want to make sure the look is balanced.

3. Stitch around the motifs, using a 3mm straight stitch.

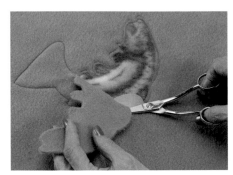

4. Working from the solid fleece side, use appliqué scissors to trim away the solid layer only from within the stitched motif. Trim close to the stitching line.

Nancy's Note

If you are using an all-over print with many motifs to choose from, it is sometimes difficult to decide which motifs to use. I find it a great help to lay the fleece on the floor, print-side up. I place pieces of paper on top of the motifs, designating which ones to outline stitch. I can easily move the papers around, changing motifs until I get a balanced look. Then I pin the paper pieces to the motifs so I can see which are the "chosen ones" when I get to the sewing machine.

Nancy's Note

Decide whether the motif outline stitching should be right on the motif edge or outside the motif edge. The only way to know is to stitch a few samples and see how they look.

When you trim away the solid fleece layer within the stitching outline, a tiny bit of fleece remains close to the stitching line, encroaching on the print. If you sew exactly on the print outline, that tiny bit of encroaching fleece crowds the motif. If you align the outer edge of your presser foot alongside the motif's outer edge, your outline stitching will be approximately ¼" away from the motif edge. If the two fleece colors are close, you will find the trimmed motif more visible if your stitching line is at least ¼" from the motif outer edge. When the solid side is trimmed, the ground color surrounding the motif will act as a narrow border to visually frame the motif.

There is no right or wrong. It is a matter of which method best complements the motif.

Blunt-Edge Appliqué Technique

Fleece is a wonderful choice for appliqué. Use fleece for the appliqué itself. Since it does not ravel, there is no need to finish the edges!

There are two ways to make a fleece appliqué: the Cut-and-Stitch Method or the Stitch-and-Cut Method.

Cut-and-Stitch Method

In the Cut-and-Stitch Method, you simply cut out the appliqué shape first and then edge stitch the cutout appliqué in place. Choose this method when the shape has simple outer edges—easy to stitch along the edge.

1. Use sharp scissors to cut out the appliqué shape from solid or print fleece.
2. Spray the wrong side of the fleece appliqué lightly with a temporary spray adhesive.
3. Adhere appliqué in place.
4. Edge stitch appliqué to secure.

Stitch-and-Cut Method

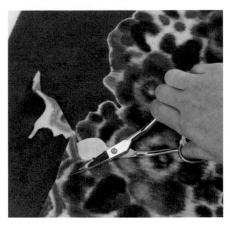

In the Stitch-and-Cut Method, you use a patch of fleece that encompasses the motif, stitch the outline of the appliqué and then trim the excess fleece close to the stitching line. Choose this method for a "busier" motif outline where edge stitching may not be as easy to do.

1. Take a patch of fleece that encompasses the appliqué motif.
2. Stitch the perimeter of the motif, securing the appliqué fabric to the base fabric.
3. Use appliqué scissors to trim excess fleece close to the stitching line.

In the examples for both methods, I used a print fleece for the motif. However, you could just as easily make your appliqué from a solid-colored fleece, as in the Double-Sided Heart Appliqué Blanket, page 38. Use Clover Mesh Transfer Canvas and water-soluble pencils to draw your own motif onto solid-colored fleece. (Refer to Mesh Transfer Canvas, page 4.)

Since it is the appliqué itself that does not ravel (because it is fleece) you can apply your fleece appliqué to any fabric!

Coordinating Print Blanket

If you are lucky enough to find coordinating prints, use them together to make a cozy double-layer blanket. Besides warding off the winter chill, such a blanket adds a classy touch to the room.

Choose the subtler of the two prints to make a coordinating pillow.

This print looks best with all four sides of the blanket fringed. Removing the corners eliminates the dilemma of how to "fringe around the corner."

MATERIALS NEEDED

Throw (54" x 60"): 1½ yards fleece for each layer

Blanket (60" x 72"): 2 yards fleece for each layer

Throw/Blanket Directions

1. Cut the two fleeces to the desired size.

2. Arrange the fleece layers with wrong sides together.

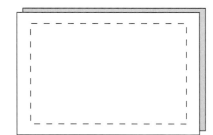

3. Sew the fleece layers together, as shown, using a 3" to 5" seam allowance (whatever depth you want the fringe to be).

4. Cut out all four corners, trimming away squares equal to the fringe length. (Trim away 3" square corners for 3" fringe, 4" corners for 4" fringe, etc.)

5. Following the Quick Fringe Technique directions on pages 7, make fringe-cuts the desired width on all four sides of the blanket, fringing both layers at once. Use the stitching line as a guide for the fringe depth.

Pillow Directions

Refer to page 45 for materials and step-by-steps for making the 14" pillow.

Nancy's Note

If you have a quilt bar accessory for your machine, use it as a stitching guide for the seamlines. (A quilt bar is not just for quilting.)

MATERIALS NEEDED

Throw (54" x 60"): 1½ yards fleece for each layer

Blanket (60" x 72"): 2 yards fleece for each layer

Blanket/Throw Directions

1. Cut two coordinating pieces of fleece to the desired size.

2. Place the fleece layers *wrong* sides together and pin to secure.

3. Place pins at each "to-be-fringed" side of the blanket to designate the end of the fringe-cuts (3" to 5" from the end of the blanket, depending on how long you want the fringe to be).

4. Sew the blanket layers together on the long sides, as shown, using a ½" seam allowance. Pivot at the pin marks to sew across the sides to be fringed.

5. Use a rotary cutter to trim the blanket close to the long unfringed seamline, extending the cut all the way to both ends of the blanket.

6. Retrue the ends to be fringed, if necessary.

7. Following the Quick Fringe Technique directions on page 7, use the stitching line as a guide for the fringe depth. Fringe both layers at once.

8. Refer to page 10 for Reverse Appliqué directions to add the fish motifs to the blanket.

Pillow Directions

Refer to page 42 for materials and step-by-steps for making the 16" pillow, as well as page 11 for Blunt-Edge Appliqué directions for the pillow front.

Appliquéd Blanket and Pillow with Multiple Techniques

This blanket and pillow combo really takes advantage of fleece's nonravel characteristic. The fish motifs on the solid side of the blanket are reverse appliqués. The fish motifs on the pillow front are blunt-edge appliqués. The blanket is finished with quick fringe, while the pillow is finished with fat piping.

Bunny Ear Blanket

The bunny ears edge finish is a clever and charming quick fringe edge finish that looks like bunny ears on the right side and twisted braid on the wrong side. The key to successful bunny ears is a tiny slit. Read on and you'll see what I mean.

The dimensions can vary. The fringe can be cut longer and wider for slightly different effects. (Longer fringe may result in a flop-eared bunny!) Experiment on a scrap of fleece first.

MATERIALS NEEDED

Fleece yardage sufficient to make blanket size desired

36" square or 36" x 45": 1 yard

45" square or 45" x 60": 1¼ yards

Note: Take into account that 4" will be used to make the bunny ears.

Directions

1. Cut a baby blanket to the desired size.

2. Cut out 2" squares from all four of the blanket corners.

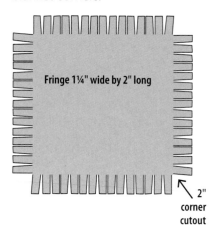

Fringe 1¼" wide by 2" long

2" corner cutout

3. Quick fringe the blanket edges, cutting the fringe 1¼" wide x 2" long. (Refer to Quick Fringe Technique page 7 for directions.)

𝒩ancy's 𝒩ote

An easy way to pull the picket-fenced fringe through the tiny slit is to insert the tips of narrow serger tweezers through the slit, pinch the fringe tip and pull it through.

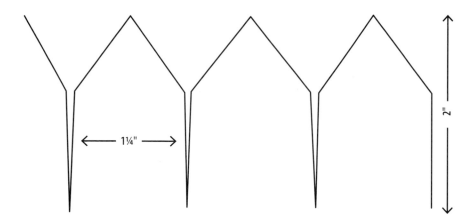

1¼"

2"

4. Cut the ends of each fringe-cut into a point, as shown. I call this "picket fencing." Don't bother to measure; just cut the fringe ends into points. If one point looks a little lopsided, simply re-cut it.

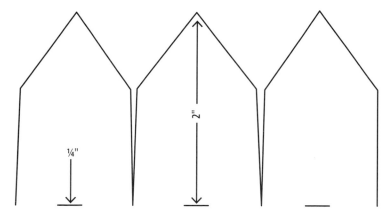

¼"

2"

5. Use a small (18mm) rotary cutter to make a *tiny* slit at the bottom center of each fringe-cut, as shown. (The slit must be tiny, just a nick, maybe ¼" wide and very narrow, so when the fringe is fed through the slit, the slit pinches the fleece, puckering it to form a bunny ear.)

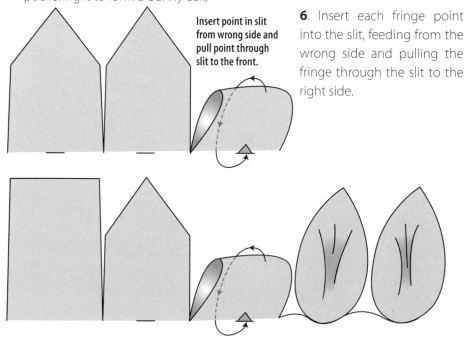

Insert point in slit from wrong side and pull point through slit to the front.

6. Insert each fringe point into the slit, feeding from the wrong side and pulling the fringe through the slit to the right side.

15

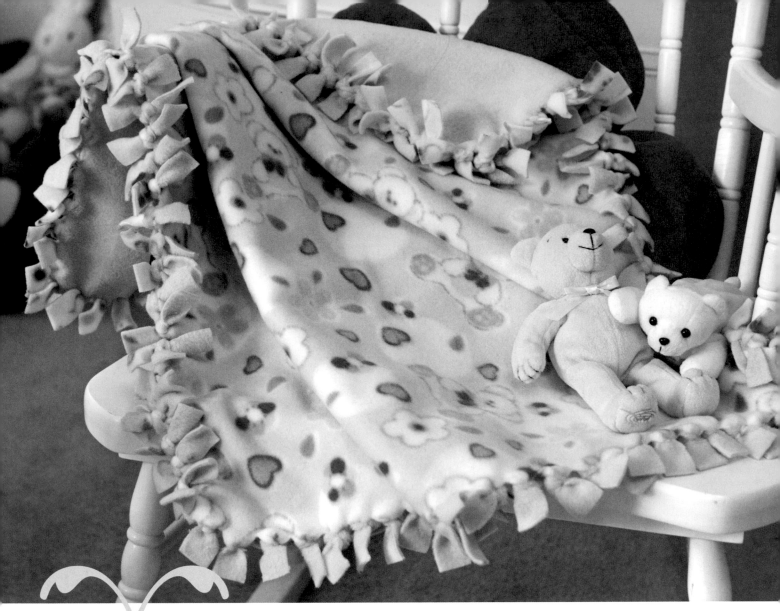

No-Sew Blanket

This is a fun alternative to sewing. (And a perfect project to make during a power outage; cut and tie by candlelight!) It's also a great take-along project to keep hands busy during long road trips.

MATERIALS NEEDED

Main fleece: 1½ yards
Contrast fleece: 1½ yards

No-Sew Guidelines

- Begin with two square cuts of fleece.
- Cut blanket layers 3" larger on all sides (6" total dimension) than the desired finished blanket. For example:
    - 60" square beginning fleece size yields a 54" square finished blanket
    - 54" square beginning fleece size yields a 48" square finished blanket

    The baby blanket shown is 45" square (finished), so both layers were initially cut 51" square, which is 6" larger all around.

16

Directions

1. Cut both fleece layers to size (6" larger than the desired finished size).

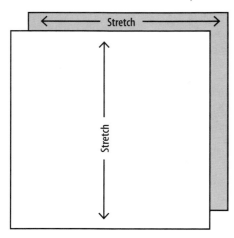

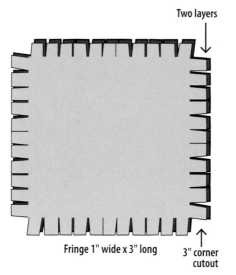

Two layers

Fringe 1" wide x 3" long

3" corner cutout

2. Place the fleece layers *wrong* sides together (finished position), *offsetting* the direction of most stretch in the layers.

3. Cut out 3" squares from all four corners (the length of the fringe).

4. Quick fringe both layers at once, following the Quick Fringe Technique on page 7. Make the fringe-cuts 1" wide x 3" long.

5. Tie each fringe pair (upper and under layers) into a square knot. Snug each knot close to the blanket base to avoid large gaps between the knots.

Nancy's Note

*Offsetting the stretch factors **only** applies to no-sew projects because we are "making the fringe do some work." In other double-layer fringe projects, there's no need to address the direction of stretch because it doesn't affect the technique or the end use. We aren't stretching, pulling or tying the fringe.*

However, when making a no-sew project, the layers are arranged so that the greater degree of stretch on each layer is opposite the other layer. Because fleece is stretchy in one direction and quite stable in the other, offsetting the stretches gives one stretchy fringe-cut and one stable fringe-cut in each knot. (Two "stretchies" are hard to work with and two "stable fringe-cuts" lay flat.)

Nancy's Comment

The beauty of quick fringing both layers together is that you automatically have matching fringe pairs to tie into knots.

MATERIALS NEEDED

Square pillow form
2 fleece squares, each 6" larger than
   pillow form

Directions

1. Cut the pillow front and back 3" larger on all sides (6" total) than the desired finished pillow size. For example, for a 16" pillow form, cut the fleece 22" square. For a 14" pillow form, cut the fleece 20" square.

2. Place the fleece layers with *wrong* sides together, offsetting the direction of the most stretch in the layers.

3. Follow steps 3 through 5 in the No-Sew Blanket directions, page 16, to quick fringe the pillow layers and tie the fringes together on three sides.

4. Insert the pillow form.

5. Tie the fringe pairs on the fourth side.

No-Sew Pillow

This pillow is an easy-to-make project for those who don't sew. The flavor changes dramatically depending on the pillow size and fleece combinations you choose. Smaller pillows in little-girl colors of pink and blue are perfect for a feminine bedroom. Large pillows in earth tones make great den floor pillows. Large pillows made in school colors, with longer ties and perhaps school letters or a sports appliqué, make great team spirit builders.

MATERIALS NEEDED

(for 51" x 65" finished size)
Solid Color 1 (orange): 1½ yards
Solid Color 2 (pink): 1½ yards

Directions

1. Cut the fleece, as follows:
- 32 Color 1 (orange) 9" squares
- 31 Color 2 (pink) 9" squares

2. Cut out 1" corner squares from all the fleece squares.

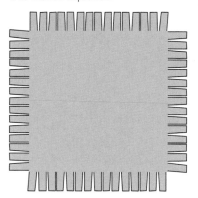

3. Quick fringe all sides of all the squares. Make the fringe-cuts ½" wide and 1" long. (Refer to page 7 for directions.)

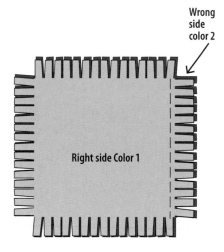

4. With *wrong* sides together, place a Color 1 square on top of a Color 2 square. Sew the squares together along the right side edge, stitching from corner cutout to corner cutout, as shown. Be careful not to catch any fringe in the seamline.

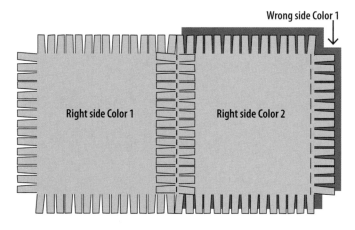

5. With *wrong* sides together, place the just sewn Color 1-Color 2 pair on top of the next Color 1 square. Sew the squares together along the right edge, sewing from corner cutout to corner cutout.

6. Refer to the layout diagram and continue adding squares as in steps 4 and 5 to finish the top row.

7. Refer to the layout diagram and sew the second through the ninth rows in the same manner.

8. With *wrong* sides together, pin and stitch the top row to the second row, matching the seamlines. Be careful not to catch any fringe in the stitching.

9. Sew the remaining rows together to complete the quilt.

Simple Rag Quilt

The quick-fringe-before-you-sew method is much easier than the scissors-clip-after-you-sew method.

1	2	1	2	1	2	1
2	1	2	1	2	1	2
1	2	1	2	1	2	1
2	1	2	1	2	1	2
1	2	1	2	1	2	1
2	1	2	1	2	1	2
1	2	1	2	1	2	1
2	1	2	1	2	1	2
1	2	1	2	1	2	1

Layout Diagram
Layout Key
1 = Color 1
2 = Color 2

Kwik Sew pattern #3284 Misses' & Girls' Ponchos

Striped fleece: 7/8* to 1 1/8* yards (per pattern envelope)

Coordinating solid color fleece (for border trim): 1/4 yard

Olfa scallop blade rotary cutter

June Tailor Fancy Fleece ruler

*Save the leftover ombre stripe, as it makes a great beaded scarf. See page 32.

Nancy's Notes

This is a small-scale poncho. I think it works best for young girls and small women.

Important note: The stripes in a fleece print may run either on the crossgrain or on the straight of grain. The direction of the stripes on the finished poncho depends upon the direction of the stripes on the printed fleece. Both ways look terrific. I just mention this to save potential confusion if your stripes don't match to the pattern envelope's picture.

If the stripes run on the straight of grain (parallel to the selvage), the striped poncho will look like the model garment and the pattern envelope.

If the stripes run on the crossgrain (from selvage to selvage), the stripes on the poncho will run the opposite direction.

Double-Scalloped Poncho

When sewing with fleece, it is easy to use a commercial pattern and add your "signature touch." This poncho is the perfect example of that concept. I called it the Double-Scalloped Poncho because we are using the scallop decorative rotary blade to cut the poncho and then using the dramatic scallop edge of the Fancy Fleece ruler to make scallop border trim underlay around the outer edges of the poncho.

Directions

1. Cut the striped fleece for poncho per pattern directions, view B.

2. Cut out the poncho using a straight-edge rotary blade or scissors.

3. Using the scallop rotary blade, trim ¼" from all the outer edges of the poncho, leaving a scalloped edge.

4. Cut contrasting fleece for the scallop border into two 4" x 60" strips.

5. Using the Fancy Fleece ruler, cut the large scallop along one long side of each strip.

6. Sew poncho per Kwik Sew view B directions, steps 1 through 4.

7. Begin construction of the scallop border underlay at center front point:

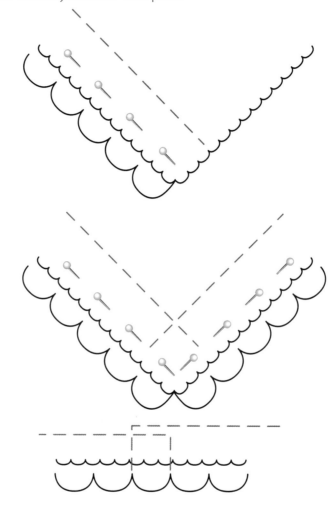

    a. With right sides facing up, slip scallop border strip under the scalloped poncho edge, having the beginning of one scallop even with center front poncho point. Place cut edge of the poncho approximately ⅜" above the slit of the large scallop on the border, as shown. Pin.

    b. Using a second contrasting strip, repeat for opposite side of poncho front. Pin.

    c. When necessary to "piece" scallop border, overlap one scallop with the new strip, as shown, pin and continue. (For one scallop, that area will be a double layer.)

    d. At center back, arrange scallops (overlap), as necessary, to accommodate point.

8. Topstitch poncho to scallop border, stitching ¼" from edge of the poncho.

9. Topstitch a second line of stitching ¼" away from the first stitching line.

10. Trim the excess fleece on the scallop border close to the stitching line.

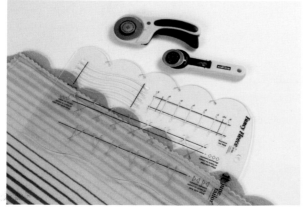

Patchwork Scarf

This pretty decorative-edged scarf is one of those projects that looks more difficult than it is. Fleece's nonravel characteristic, teamed with lapped seam construction, a decorative scallop rotary blade and wash-away basting tape, make this scarf quick and easy to sew. (Hmm… Does this give you an idea for a different way to approach crazy patch projects?)

MATERIALS NEEDED

Fleece Color 1 (pink): ¼ yard
Fleece Color 2 (blue): ¼ yard
Fleece Color 3 (white): ¼ yard
Wash-away basting tape
Scallop rotary blade
Thread to blend with all

Directions

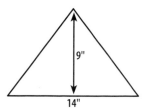

1. Draw a triangle pattern piece 14" wide at the base and 9" high.
2. Cut four pink triangles, three blue triangles and three white triangles.
3. Place all the triangles right-side up on a table. (Pull gently in the direction of the most stretch. The fleece will curl toward the *wrong* side.)
4. Build the patchwork scarf from left to right, with the left patch always overlapping the patch on its right.

a. Place a strip of basting tape on the left edge of the blue triangle.

b. Overlap a pink triangle on the blue triangle by ½" and adhere.

c. Stitch the layers together using a wavy or serpentine stitch to complement the scalloped edge. Align the right edge of the presser foot to the top of the rounded scallop. (It's always best to test stitch on a scrap first.)

d. Place basting tape on the left edge of a white triangle.

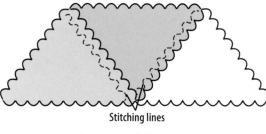

Stitching lines

e. Overlap the pink/blue segment on the white triangle and adhere.

f. Continue building the scarf, ending with a pink triangle.

MATERIALS NEEDED

Kwik Sew pattern #3022 (ladies) view A
   or B or #2249 (boys and girls) view A
Print fleece: per pattern
Solid fleece: per pattern
Scallop, wave or straight rotary blades

Reversible Vest with Reverse Appliqué

This easy-to-sew vest features a blunt-edge finish. The woman's vest exposed seam allowance is trimmed using the Olfa wave blade, the girl's vest is trimmed using the Olfa scallop blade and the boy's vest is trimmed using the Olfa straight-edge rotary blade. All three vests are embellished with reverse appliqué. Since a reversible vest is essentially two vests sewn together, the yardage requirements are the same for both the print layer and the solid color layer.

Directions

1. Cut out the vest fronts and back pieces from the print and solid fleeces.

Important:

- Cut the back piece from pattern #2249 on the fold to eliminate a back seam.
- Place the right front vest of the print fleece (as when wearing) in such a way as to appropriately place a print motif for making the reverse appliqué.

2. Sew the shoulder seams, side seams and collar (if applicable) of the print vest layer color.

3. Sew the shoulder seams, side seams and collar (if applicable) of the solid-colored vest layer.

4. Place the two vests *wrong* sides together (finished position) and pin.

5. Sew the vests together around all the outer edges and armholes using a ½" seam allowance. (**Note:** This is a wider seam allowance than indicated in the pattern directions. When you trim off the exposed seam allowance, you will "net out" at the original ¼" seam allowance.)

6. Using the decorative wave or scallop blade (for the ladies and girls) or straight blade (for the boys), trim the exposed seam allowance, cutting ¼" away from the seamline.

Nancy's Note

Caution: If you are using the scallop blade in step 6, make a test cut on a fleece scrap to make sure the blade is inserted correctly for a scallop rather than a peaked cut edge.

7. With print side facing out, choose a motif (or motifs) for reverse appliqué on one vest front. Stitch. Trim solid layer from within the stitching lines. Refer to Reverse Appliqué Technique directions on page 10.

Nancy's Note

The boy's print did not offer any motif for reverse appliqué, so I made my own! I used Clover Mesh Transfer Canvas and water-soluble pencils (see page 4 to trace and draw angular motifs on the solid side of the vest left front. (It's easier to see drawn lines on the solid fleece, rather than on the print fleece side.)

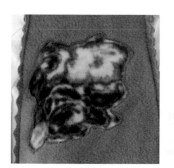
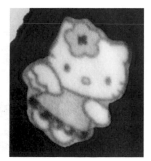

Chenille Tote

This easy tote can serve many purposes. It can be a simple soft carryall for shopping, a great storage bag for yarn and knitting needles, an easy place to store all the items you need to take to a sewing class, or when made from a kid-friendly fabric, a fun bag to take on overnights.

MATERIALS NEEDED

Fleece print: ½ yard

Fleece solid: ⅝ yard

Stiff heavyweight sew-in stabilizer (for bottom base): ¼ yard

Draw cord or ribbon: 1¼ yards

Buttons, cord locks or pony beads as desired (to decorate draw cord ends)

Olfa Chenille Cutter

Directions

1. Cut from print fleece:

- 8½" circle (for the base)
- 30" x 18" (for one side panel, with the stretch in the length)

2. Cut from solid fleece:

- 8½" circle (for the base)
- 30" x 20" (for one side panel, with the stretch in the length)

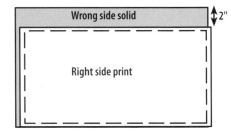

3. Place the print rectangle against the solid panel with wrong sides together. Position the print panel on the solid so 2" of the solid panel extends above the print panel. Baste the pieces together.

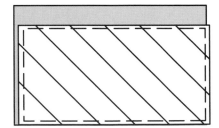

4. On the right side of the print panel, draw 45-degree angle lines, spaced approximately 3" apart, as shown.

5. Use the drawn lines as a guide to stitch rows ⅜" apart. Sew from the top basted edge to the lower edge, filling the fabric piece.

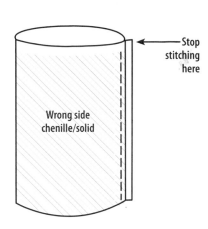

Stop
stitching
here

Wrong side
chenille/solid

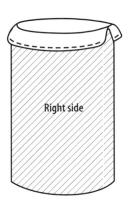

Right side

6. Remove the basting stitches. Use Olfa Chenille cutter to slash open the channels on the print side.

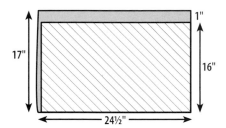

1"

17"

16"

24½"

7. Refer to the illustration to cut chenilled rectangle.

8. Cut a circle 8" in diameter from stabilizer.

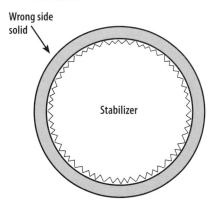

Wrong side solid

Stabilizer

9. Using a wide and long zigzag stitch, center and stitch the stabilizer to the wrong side of the solid base.

10. Sew the print base to the solid base with wrong sides together (sandwiching the stabilizer), using a ¼" seam allowance.

11. With right sides together, sew the chenille side panel into a circle, using a ¼" seam allowance. Sew from the bottom of the panel up to, *but not through*, the solid extension, as shown.

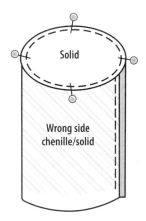

Solid

Wrong side
chenille/solid

12. With right sides of the print together, sew the side panel to the stabilized base as follows:

- Divide the base perimeter into quarters and mark with pins.
- Divide the chenilled edge of the side panel into quarters and mark with pins.
- Match the quarter marks of the base to the quarter marks of the side panel.
- Sew the base to the side panel using ¼" seam allowances.

13. At the top edge of the tote, fold the solid facing (1" extension) onto the print fleece, encasing the raw edge of the chenille and at the same time forming a casing for the draw cord. Edge stitch the facing to the tote bag, as shown, beginning and ending at the unsewn ends of the folded-over facing.

14. Insert decorative ribbon or cord in the casing and cut it to the desired length. Add decorative beads, buttons or cord locks, as desired, to the ends of the draw cord.

MATERIALS NEEDED

(depending upon width of scarf
  desired)
Print fleece: ¼ to ⅓ yard
Solid color coordinate fleece: ¼ to
  ⅓ yard
Appliqué scissors
Olfa decorative rotary blade
  (optional)

Directions

1. Cut fleece layers the desired width.
2. Place the fleece layers wrong sides together (the finished position). Stitch the layers together as follows:
   - For fringed ends: Stitch long sides with ½" seam allowance and short ends with 5" seam allowance. Trim close to stitching lines on long sides. Quick fringe the end. (Refer to the Quick Fringe Technique directions on page 7.)
   - For decorative exposed seams: Cut scarf ends to desired shape (pointed, squared, angled). Stitch scarf outer edges with ½" seam allowance. Trim exposed seam allowance using the Olfa wave or scallop decorative rotary blade. Trim ¼" away from seamline.
3. Stitch around the print fleece motifs using a 3mm straight stitch.
4. Use appliqué scissors to trim out the solid fleece layer only from within the motif stitching lines to reveal the print layer peeking through.

Easy Reverse Appliqué Scarves

Choose a fleece print with a relatively simple design motif, team it with a complementary solid and you are ready to go! You can sprinkle the reverse appliqués the length of the scarf or simply use at one end.

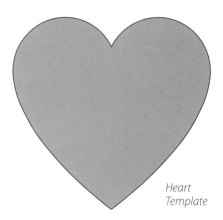

MATERIALS NEEDED

Lap blanket: 1 yard each of two contrasting fleeces

Blanket: 1½ to 2 yards each of two contrasting fleeces

Regular thread to match each color

Clover Mesh Transfer Canvas

Clover water-soluble pencils

Appliqué scissors

Heart Template

Heart Blanket with Reverse Appliqué

This blanket is designed for mid- to heavier-weight solid-colored fleece.

Directions

1. Trim selvages from fleece. Measure the length and width of the fleeces to plan for the number of motifs to be placed in each direction.
   - Allow for ½" seam allowance around all the edges.
   - Allow for 5" corner boxes (twice as large as border boxes).
   - Allow for 2½" border boxes.
   - Trim the length or width, as necessary, to match the motif box measurement needs.

2. Place the fleeces *wrong* sides together. Pin them together at a 90-degree angle to the cut edges.

3. With matching threads in the needle and bobbin (two different colors, matching each fleece color), sew a ½" seam allowance around the entire blanket.

4. Using a rotary cutter and ruler, trim to ¼" away from the seamline on all sides.

5. Sew a 5" box in each corner by drawing a 5" box in each corner using a water-soluble pencil and stitching the box.

6. Attach a quilt bar (spacer bar, edge guide, etc.) to your machine and sew one long 2½" border along the short edges and a long double-border (two 2½" rows) along the long edges.

7. Sew cross seams to form 2½" boxes in all borders.

8. Trace a heart on the matte side of the Clover Mesh Transfer Canvas.

9. Referring to the photo for placement, trace a heart in every other 2½" box, leaving the alternate boxes plain. Trace three hearts in the 5" corner boxes. For best visibility, trace the heart onto the darkest fleece color.

10. Stitch around each heart.

11. Use appliqué scissors to trim just the top layer to reveal the contrast underneath. Trim all the hearts on one side. (Only the outline stitching of the heart will be visible on the opposing side.)

12. Trim all the plain boxes on the other side. (Only the outlined stitching of the boxes will be visible on the opposing side.) Results: Contrasting hearts on one side of the blanket and contrasting boxes on the other.

Crusher Hat and Fringed Scarf

This warm, comfortable hat is so easy to make. The reverse appliqués are completed before construction. And the fringed scarf is the perfect companion to the hat. When I made my first one, I couldn't decide which color to trim from within the tree motifs at the ends of the scarf, so I decided to trim opposite colors from each end!

MATERIALS NEEDED

Hat: ¼ yard each of two contrasting solid fleece colors (must have 25 percent stretch)
Scarf: ¼ yard each of two contrasting solid fleece colors
Regular thread to match both colors
Clover Mesh Transfer Canvas
Clover water-soluble pencils
Appliqué scissors
Size 16 sewing machine needle

Hat Directions

Note: Use ¼" seam allowance throughout.

1. From each of the two contrasting solid fleece colors, cut:
   - 8¼" diameter circle for the top of the hat

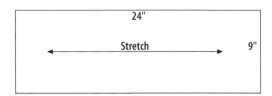

   - 9" x 24" band (with the greater stretch going in the length)

2. With right sides together, sew the short ends of each band together, forming a circle.

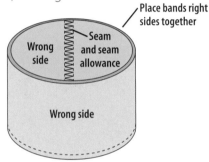

3. With right sides together and matching the center back seams, sew the bands together along one long edge. Turn right-side out.

4. Using the Clover Mesh Transfer Canvas and the Tree Template, trace and draw the tree motif at the center front of the hat band.

5. With matching threads in the needle and bobbin, straight stitch the tree outline. (To determine the tree placement, roll back 3" of contrasting cuff. Place the top of the tree toward the finished seam. Unroll and stitch.)

6. On the contrasting side of hat band, use appliqué scissors to trim one layer only from the center of the tree.

7. Turn the band to the finished position (with the rolled-up cuff showing the tree and sides lying smoothly against each other). Trim approximately ¾" from the top raw edge of the outer layer to make the raw edges even. (The contrast color uses more than the main color in the roll-back.)

8. "Spot" baste circle hat tops with wrong sides together.

30

*Broken lines show spot basting.
Outline stitch tree motif and trim away top
fleece layer.*

9. Trace, draw and outline stitch a single tree (or multiple trees) and trim one layer from the main color to reveal the contrasting underneath. (The hat top shows a contrasting tree on the main color. The hat band cuff shows the main color tree on the contrast color.)

10. With right sides together, use a 4mm stitch length and size 16 needle to sew the hat tops to the hat band. If the hat top features a single tree, place the tree top pointing toward the center back seam. Repeat the stitching with a serger, if desired. (Adjust the serger stitch length, pressure and needles to accommodate the bulk.)

Fringed Scarf Directions

1. Cut each fleece layer 9" x 60".
2. Place the scarves *wrong* sides together. Using a conventional sewing machine, stitch the long edges with a ½" seam allowance, leaving 5" unstitched at each short end for fringing.
3. Use a rotary cutter to trim to ¼" away from the seamline.
4. Quick fringe 5" at each short end, making ½" cuts. (Refer to the Quick Fringe Technique directions on page 7.) Quick fringe both layers at once.
5. Using Mesh Transfer Canvas and water-soluble pencil, trace and draw three trees staggered above the fringed ends at both ends of the scarf.
6. With matching threads in the needle and bobbin, straight stitch the tree outlines.
7. Trim one layer only from the center of the trees on one side of the scarf (revealing the contrasting fleece).
8. Trim the opposite color at the other end of the scarf.

Tree Template

Fringed Scarf with School Spirit

This scarf is a great gift for teens and college men and women! Choose the school's colors for each layer of fleece.

1. Stitch and quick fringe the scarf ends just as in steps 1 through 3 of the Fringed Scarf directions.
2. Using a collegiate or serif font from your computer, enlarge and print the school letters to fit proportionally between the 8" scarf seamlines. (A three-letter sequence fills an area approximately 6" to 7" wide x 2½" to 3" high.)
3. Using Clover Mesh Transfer Canvas and water-soluble pencil, trace and draw school letters at one end of the scarf. Flip the traced canvas over and then trace the reversed letters on the opposite end of the scarf.
4. With matching threads in the needle and bobbin, straight stitch the letter outlines.
5. Trim one layer of fleece from the centers of the letters, making sure the letters read correctly at both ends!

𝒩ancy's 𝒩ote

Be sure to plan first. You are reversing the colors trimmed at one end versus the other. Flip the traced transfer canvas over before tracing the opposing end. (In order to have the letters read correctly when trimmed.)

MATERIALS NEEDED

Kwik Sew pattern #3022 Misses Vest

Vest: 1 yard fleece

Scarf: ¼ yard fleece

6mm x 9mm pony beads

Size US9/1.25mm metal crochet hook (to apply beads)

Vest Directions

1. Cut out the vest fronts and back, making the following changes:
   - Use view B neckline and view A length.
   - Add another 5" length to view A's lower edge.
2. Quick fringe the lower edge of the vest fronts and back with cuts ⅝" wide x 5" long. (Refer to the Quick Fringe Technique directions on page 7.)
3. Sew the side seams and the shoulder seams.
4. Turn under ½" at the armhole edges and topstitch to secure.
5. Turn under ½" at the center front and neck edges. Topstitch to secure.

Scarf Directions

1. Cut the scarf fleece to 9" x 60". Angle-cut the ends into blunt points, if desired.
2. Quick fringe each short end with cuts ⅝" wide x 5" long.

Beading Directions

1. Stack a few pony beads on the metal crochet hook.
2. Hook a fringed end of fleece and slide a bead (or multiple beads) onto the fringe.
3. Tie a single knot at the fringe end and slide the bead down to the knot.

Beaded Vest and Scarf

This is a fun project to play with. For an interesting effect, vary the number of beads on the fringe-cuts— one bead, two beads, three beads, two beads, one bead, etc.

Nancy's Caution

Don't use beaded fringe on items for babies or toddlers. The beads could be pulled off and swallowed.

MATERIALS NEEDED

Kwik Sew pattern #3219, view B

Print fleece: per view B (1⅝ to 2⅛ yards)

Solid fleece: same as print fleece

Olfa scallop decorative rotary blade

June Tailor Fancy Fleece ruler

4. Sew around the neck opening and the slit using a skimpy ⅜" seam allowance. Pivot at bottom of the slit.

5. Sew outer edge of poncho using 1½" seam allowance.

6. Use the Fancy Fleece ruler scalloped edge to trim the exposed outer seam allowance, as follows:

   a. Begin trimming at one side edge on the back of the poncho.

   b. Align the top edge of teardrop opening on the ruler to the stitched seamline and cut scallops following the manufacturer's directions.

Close-up of finished large scalloped edge.

   c. The teardrop openings at the top of each scallop on the ruler allow for the rotary blade to completely cut to the point of the scallop.

   d. Since you are cutting on a curved line, you will need to constantly slide and realign the teardrops to be next to the stitching line.

   e. Stop cutting scallops approximately 12" from your starting point. Measure the remaining space left and compare to the measurements of the scallops. Adjust the remaining scallops as necessary (a little generous or a little skimpy) to be able to end with a complete scallop.

7. Use the scallop rotary blade to trim the exposed seam allowance around neck edge and slit opening. Caution: Do a test cut first to make sure the blade is inserted correctly to result in a scalloped edge (rather than the opposing peaked edge).

Close-up of finished small scalloped edge around the neckline.

Reversible Poncho

This quick-and-easy pattern was designed as a single-layer, no-sew project. However, as you can see here, it is very easy to make it warmer and reversible (double-layer) and add some fancy edges. (The neck opening is trimmed with the scallop rotary blade and poncho outer edges are cut into larger scallops using the Fancy Fleece ruler.)

Directions

1. Cut out one print fleece poncho per view B.

2. Cut out one solid fleece poncho per view B.

3. Place ponchos *wrong* sides together (finished position), matching neckline openings, slits and outer edges. Pin.

Reverse Hem Blanket

This baby blanket again takes advantage of fleece's nonravel characteristic to make a "binding" edge finish and "cheater's mitered corners." The blanket front can be a fleece, a woven flannel or a fun novelty fabric that sheds because the cut edges will be wrapped and encased by the back fleece layer. If choosing blanket front fabric that shrinks with laundering (like cotton flannel), make sure to pre-treat that fabric before sewing. Fleece does not need to be pre-treated.

MATERIALS NEEDED

Fleece for blanket front (print, solid or novelty): 1¼ yards

Fleece for blanket back and reverse hem (print or solid): 1⅜ yards

Straight or decorative blade rotary cutter

Nancy's Note

For larger (or smaller) blankets, increase (or decrease) both the blanket front and blanket back yardage requirements accordingly. Cut the back layer 4" larger than the front layer.

Directions

Note: Directions are for 45" square blanket size.

1. Cut blanket front 45" square.

2. Cut blanket back 49" square, using a straight or decorative rotary blade.

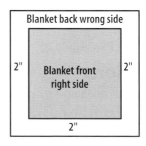

3. Lay the fleece back on a table, wrong-side up. (To find the right side, gently pull on the cut edge of the crossgrain, which is the direction of most stretch. Fleece will curl toward the wrong side.) Center the blanket front, right-side up, on top of the fleece blanket back, leaving

a 2" fleece back border extending beyond all the blanket front edges. If necessary, trim the fleece edges so you have an even border.

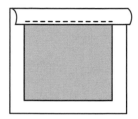

4. Fold a 2" fleece hem along the top edge of the blanket, encasing the blanket front raw edge. Pin the hem in place, with the pins perpendicular to the hem edge. Beginning and ending at the blanket front edges, edge stitch the fleece hem.

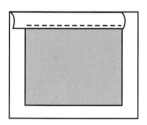

5. Trim the upper right corner of the blanket back *hem* only.

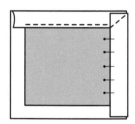

6. Fold and pin a 2" fleece hem along the right edge of the blanket, encasing the blanket front raw edge. Stitch from corner to corner (this is the cheater's mitered corner).

7. Trim the excess fleece corner wedge piece.

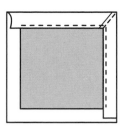

8. Edge stitch the fleece side hem, stopping at the edge of the blanket front.

9. Repeat this sequence to miter the remaining three corners and edge stitch the hems for the finished appearance shown.

Finished mitered corners and hems.

MATERIALS NEEDED

1 to 1¼ yards fleece

¼ yard cuts of pastel fleece solid colors

Clover Mesh Transfer Canvas

Clover water-soluble pencils

Appliqué scissors

Double-Sided Heart Appliqué Blanket

This sweet baby blanket offers "back-to-back" appliqués. Each heart appliqué has an exactly matching counterpart on the opposite side of the blanket. The blunt-edge method of appliqué makes this quick, easy and a perfect match every time.

Blunt-Edge Appliqué Tips for Success

Refer to page 11 for two different methods of Blunt-Edge Appliqué. This delightful Double-Sided Heart Appliqué Blanket uses both!

This double-layer appliqué idea comes from Jeanine Twigg (the Snap Source snap expert, embroidery expert and author of the *Embroidery Machine Essentials* series, and a lover of sewing with fleece).

Although I feature this technique in soft, pretty baby colors, this idea would work beautifully in many other themes:

- Earthy colors with double appliqué leaves
- Soccer balls, footballs, baseballs or basketballs sewn in team colors

- Sky blue fleece with stars, clouds and an occasional crescent moon

Whatever you choose, just remember to keep the motifs simple and fairly basic.

Want to venture beyond blankets? This idea would work beautifully on a reversible vest; just change the colors of the appliqués for two different looks!

Directions

1. Cut the fleece to the size blanket you wish to make (36" square, 36" x 45" or 45" square).

2. Finish the edges with a straight or wavy blade rotary cutter, serger finish using a pretty yarn or quick fringe.

3. Determine the placement of the heart appliqués.

4. For *each* double-appliqué, cut *two pieces* of fleece for the appliqués at least 2" larger all around than the finished appliqué. For the heart motif given here, the appliqué fleece pieces need to be at least 8" square.

5. Draw a heart motif on the right side of one fleece appliqué piece, using Clover Mesh Transfer Canvas and water-soluble pencils. (Refer to page 4.)

6. For each double-sided heart appliqué:

   a. Pin a traced heart fleece piece to the blanket where desired.

   b. Pin a matching color plain piece of fleece on the opposite side of the blanket with the wrong side of the appliqué piece against the blanket, sandwiching the blanket between. (This is why the appliqué pieces are larger than you really need. The alignment is not exact.)

7. Straight stitch the heart motif using a 3mm stitch length. (You are stitching through three layers: traced heart appliqué piece, blanket and plain appliqué piece.)

8. Use appliqué scissors to trim the excess fleece from the outer edges of the stitching on both appliqué pieces, trimming close to the stitching line.

9. Repeat sewing the sets of appliqués until the blanket is embellished as you like.

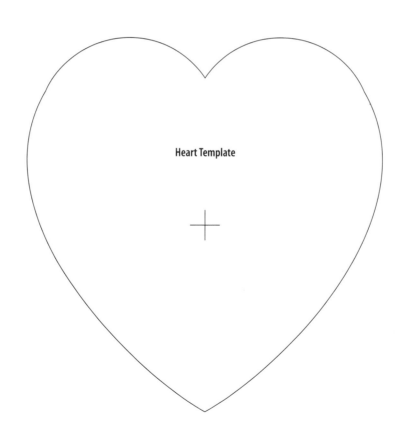

Heart Template

MATERIALS NEEDED

Throw (54" x 60"): 1½ yards plus
   extra for pillow appliqués
Blanket (60" x 72"): 2 yards plus extra
   for pillow appliqués
6mm x 9mm pony beads: 2 gross
US9/1.25 metal crochet hook (to
   apply pony beads)

Throw Directions

1. Cut the fleece to the desired size.

2. Quick fringe two opposing ends of
the throw. Make the fringe-cuts ⅝"
wide x 5" long. (Refer to the Quick
Fringe Technique directions on
page 7.)

Nancy's Note

*You are cutting the fringe a little
wider than ½" so it doesn't get distorted
when you're beading the ends. Fringe-
cuts, especially those made on the
crossgrain, will stretch when pulled
through the bead holes.*

3. Using a crochet hook, place the
beads on the fringe and tie the
ends to secure. (Refer to the Beaded
Vest and Scarf, page 32, for beading
directions.)

Nancy's Note

*Don't put beads on blankets
or pillows that will be around small
children. The beads aren't secure enough
for curious minds, little hands and busy
fingers.*

Southwest Throw

*Creating this throw and
coordinating pillows has to be about
the easiest and quickest way to
freshen a room. The throw is simply
quick-fringed and finished with
pony beads for a Southwest flavor.*

Southwest Pillows

When a print doesn't offer specific motifs for appliqué, create your own! Study the fleece print and determine what elements can be used for interesting appliqué motifs or accent bands. The throw print offered a variety of blunt-edge appliqué options for the pillows. For maximum interest, vary the appliqué sizes and shapes, as well as the pillow sizes. Making the pillows "envelope-style" allows you to easily change pillow covers for different seasons or holidays.

MATERIALS NEEDED

Fleece main color solid (for pillow): ⅝ yard mid-weight fleece

Fleece contrast color (for fat piping): ⅛ yard

Fleece appliqué or accent bands cut from blanket fleece print

16" square pillow form

100/16 universal needle (for construction; see note)

Nancy's Notes

• These materials and directions are for a 16" pillow form. The requirements for different size pillow forms are given on page 45.

• Normally, you would use a 14/90 needle for construction, but when you sew the fat piping, you will be stitching through three and four layers of fleece and will need the strength of the larger-sized needle.

Directions

1. From contrast fleece color, cut one 4" x 60" trim strip for the fat piping edge finish.

2. From the main fleece color, cut one pillow front, 19" square (3" larger than the pillow form) and cut two pillow half-backs, 17½" x 12¾".

3. On the right side of the pillow front, arrange the fleece appliqués (or accent bands) as desired. Lightly spray the wrong side of the appliqués (or accent bands) with temporary adhesive spray and adhere them to the pillow front.

4. Stitch the appliqués (or accent bands) to the pillow front using one of the following methods.
   a. Using regular thread in the needle and an edge stitch or edge-joining presser foot, edge stitch the appliqués in place.
   b. With rayon thread in the needle, stitch the appliqués (or accent bands) in place. Choose a blanket stitch, lengthening and widening the stitch for a noticeable stitch. For an even bolder stitch, thread the machine with two spools of contrast rayon thread, threading both threads through the larger eye of the size 16/100 needle. Sew slowly to avoid thread loops.

5. Re-true and trim the pillow front to 17½" square (1½" larger than the pillow form).

Nancy's Note

If you have enough fleece and nap or print is not an issue, cut the 17½" in the direction of the least stretch. Since you are making an envelope-style closing on the backside of the pillow, there is less potential for distortion if it is cut this way.

Nancy's Note

If your fleece print doesn't offer defined motifs for appliqués, make one up! It can be as simple as a geometric shape that complements the flavor of the print. Notice that most of the appliqués used on the Southwest Pillows are geometric shapes.

Nancy's Note

Starting with a 19" square pillow front, then trimming to 17½" square provides a fudge factor in case the appliqués are not centered exactly or something shifts during the stitching process.

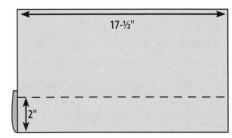

6. Turn under and topstitch 2" hems on one long edge of each half-back.

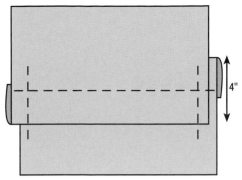

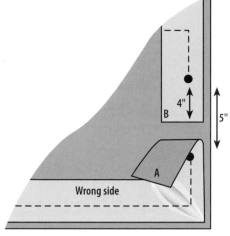

Wrong side

7. Overlap the half-back hems 4" and baste them together with ¾" seam allowances.

8. Pin the pillow front to the basted pillow half-backs with wrong sides together (finished position).

9. Place the right side of the 4" trim strip (from step 1) against the right side of the pillow front.

12. Cut the ending edge of the strip exactly 4" beyond the ending stitching.

16. Finish sewing the last 5" of the spliced trim strip to the pillow.

17. Trim away one seam allowance layer in the *overlap area only* on the half-backs to make the bulk comparable to the rest of the pillow. (Don't trim away any other seam allowance. In the following steps, when wrapping and enclosing the seam allowance, the fluffiness of the fleece "plumps" the wrap and gives a fat piping appearance.)

18. To finish the fat piping edge, wrap the trim strip to the backside, wrapping up, over and around, to encase the raw edge of the seam allowances. Trim just the tips of the pillow corners for ease in wrapping.

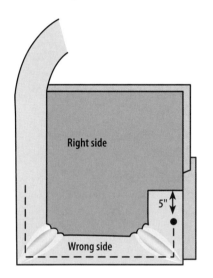

Right side

Wrong side

10. Using an *exact* ¾" seam allowance, begin sewing 5" from the end of the trim strip. (You are sewing through three layers: front, back and trim strip.) To avoid additional bulk when you splice the strip ends, begin stitching the trim strip away from the pillow back overlap area.)

11. Sew the trim strip to the outer edge of the pillow, slightly stretching the trim strip while sewing. Pivot at the corners. Stop sewing exactly 5" before the beginning stitching. (**Note:** If you don't stretch the trim slightly, you will not have enough length.)

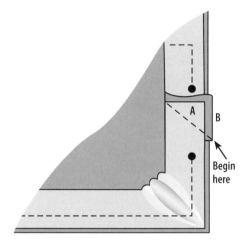

A B

Begin here

13. Lift up both unsewn ends of the trim strip. Match and pin the edges, as illustrated, with right sides together.

𝒩ancy's 𝒩ote

Pin first, check and then sew. It's easier to unpin than tear out stitching!

14. Sew A to B "on the diagonal," beginning exactly at the corner of B.

15. Before trimming the spliced strip, double-check on the right side to make sure everything looks right. Trim the seam allowance to ¼" and finger press it open.

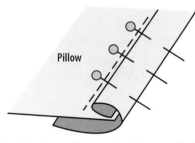

Pillow

19. Working from the front of the pillow, pin the trim strip in place, making sure the plump wrapped edges are consistent.

20. Using an edge stitch or edge-joining presser foot for precise stitch placement, stitch in the ditch on the right side of the pillow to secure the wrapped trim strip. (To stitch in the ditch, sew exactly in the seamline.) Use needle thread that matches the main fleece color (pillow) and bobbin thread that matches the contrast color (fat piping).

21. On the backside of the pillow, use appliqué scissors to cut the excess trim close to the stitching line.

22. Insert the pillow form through the flap opening.

23. *Optional:* Attach a snap, button or hook-and-loop tape to hold the envelope back closed.

Knotted Fringed Throw

Side-by-side fringe cuts tied together add a slightly different edge finish. The coordinating pillow uses the fleece print for the blunt-edge appliqué and fat piping pillow edge finish.

MATERIALS NEEDED

Throw (54" x 60"): 1½ yards plus ⅛ yard for fat piping for 16" coordinate pillow

Blanket (60" x 72"): 2 yards plus ⅛ yard for fat piping for 16" coordinate pillow*

*Buy additional print fleece for pillow appliqués.

Directions

1. Cut the fleece to the desired size.
2. Quick fringe two opposing ends of the throw. Make the fringe-cuts a generous ½" wide x 5" long. (Refer to the Quick Fringe Technique directions on page 7.)
3. Beginning at one corner, tie two side-by-side fringe cuts in a simple double-knot.

Directions for Different Pillow Sizes

The directions for construction of these coordinate pillows are exactly the same as the Southwest Pillows, page 41, except the fat piping is made using the blanket fleece print. Contrast fleece yardages listed below are for the fat piping only. Purchase enough additional fleece print for the appliqués.

Follow the construction directions for the Southwest Pillows, adjusting for different pillow form sizes as follows:

Nancy's Note

One 4" x 60" strip will make fat piping for a 14" or 16" pillow form. Two 4" x 60" strips, spliced, are needed for a pillow form 18" or larger.

20" PILLOW FORM

Main yardage: ⅔ yard

Contrast yardage: ¼ yard (for fat piping)

1. Cut two contrast strips 4" x 60" long (for fat piping).
2. Splice trim strips to make one long strip.
3. Cut the pillow front 23" square (3" larger than pillow form).
4. Cut two half-backs 21½" x 14¾".
5. Trim the pillow front to 21½" square.

18" PILLOW FORM

Main yardage: ⅝ yard

Contrast yardage: ¼ yard (for fat piping)

1. Cut two contrast strips 4" x 60" long (for fat piping).
2. Splice trim strips to make one long strip.
3. Cut the pillow front 21" square (3" larger than pillow form).
4. Cut two half-backs 19½" x 13¾".
5. Trim the pillow front to 19½" square.

14" PILLOW FORM

Main yardage: ½ yard

Contrast yardage: ⅛ yard (for fat piping)

1. Cut one contrast strip 4" x 60" long (for fat piping).
2. Cut the pillow front 17" square (3" larger than pillow form).
3. Cut two half-backs 15½" x 11¾".
4. Trim the pillow front to 15½" square.

King of the Castle Dog Bed

This is an easy bed to make for that special furry member of your household. The directions call for a 30" square pillow form, which is perfect for a medium-sized animal (or a small animal that rules a large kingdom). If you have a petite pet, refer to page 45 and choose a smaller, more appropriate pillow-form size.

MATERIALS NEEDED

Dog print fleece: 1¾ yards
Solid contrast fleece (for fat piping edge finish): ¼ yard
30" square pillow form

Directions

1. Cut pillow front 31½" square.
2. Cut two pillow half-backs 19¾" x 31½" (have the greater stretch of fleece going in the 19¾" direction).
3. Cut two piping pieces from contrast fleece 4" x 60".
4. Splice the two piping strips to make one long 4" x 120" piping strip.
5. Refer to page 42 for pillow construction.

Nancy's Notes

• *Since this is a one-way, directional print, arrange the pillow backs so the print matches the front print direction.*

• *Stretch the trim slightly when sewing the fat piping, or you will not have enough length.*

Quick Fringe Hat

This is a great way to use up those fleece leftovers that are just too big to toss away. Use the hat for secret friend gift exchanges, hostess gifts, church bazaar fundraisers, or donate to a shelter in need. Since the hat shape is pretty close to square, make sure you sew it with the stretch going "around the head" (or else it won't fit).

MATERIALS NEEDED

(per hat)

Fleece: ⅔ yard

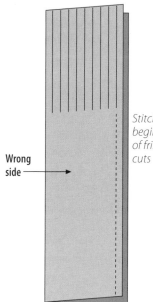

Wrong side

Stitch to beginning of fringe cuts

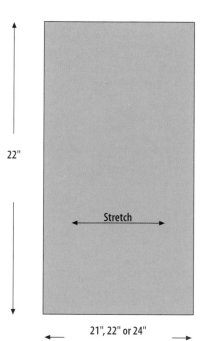

22"

Stretch

21", 22" or 24"

½" cuts

8"

Stretch

5. Sew the center back seam with a ¼" seam allowance, stitching from the unfringed short end and stopping at the fringe-cuts.

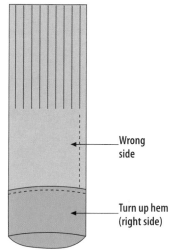

Wrong side

Turn up hem (right side)

Directions

Note: Designed for fleece with 25 percent crossgrain stretch.

1. Cut a fleece rectangle 22" high x 21" wide (small), 22" wide (medium) or 24" (large) wide, with the stretch going in the width.

2. Cut a strip of fleece ½" x 22" for the fringed tassel tie. (Cut the tie on the straight-of-grain, resulting in very little stretch in the length of the tie.)

3. Quick fringe the fleece rectangle, making fringe-cuts ½" wide x 8" deep on one short end of the rectangle. (Refer to the Quick Fringe Technique directions on page 7)

4. With right sides together, fold in half (22" x 10½", 11" or 12").

6. Turn up a 4" hem on the unfringed end and topstitch in place.

7. Tie the hat at the beginning of the fringe-cuts to form a tassel at the top of the hat.

8. When wearing, turn up the hem for a rollback band.

Finished view

Sunflower Blanket and Pillow

This blanket and pillow set is so fresh and fun, I decided it was the perfect ending to a fun-filled fleece adventure!

The directions for making this (or similar) blankets and pillows can be found throughout the book.

When you find a new fleece print suitable for home décor use, let the print determine the best way to use it in a blanket and pillow.

The direction and balance of a print frequently dictate what edge will look best fringed, whether the pillow fat piping will work best in a coordinate solid color or if it will be made from the print fabric.

Choose whatever looks best to you. There is no hard-and-fast rule.

Have fun and enjoy the adventure.

Love,